Christmas

CLASSIC RECIPES™

Publications International, Ltd.
Favorite Brand Name Recipes at www.fbnr.com

Microwave Cooking: Microwave ovens vary in wattage. Use the cooking times as guidelines and check for doneness before adding more time.

Preparation/Cooking Times: Preparation times are based on the approximate amount of time required to assemble the recipe before cooking, baking, chilling or serving. These times include preparation steps such as measuring, chopping and mixing. The fact that some preparations and cooking can be done simultaneously is taken into account. Preparation of optional ingredients and serving suggestions is not included.

Table of Contents

Joyous Beginnings

*Kick off your holiday feast with
sensational starters. Whether you're
looking for a cold appetizer or hot,
there's something to please every palate.*

Nutty Bacon Cheeseball

1 package (8 ounces) cream cheese, softened

$^1/_2$ cup milk

2 cups (8 ounces) shredded sharp cheddar cheese

2 cups (8 ounces) shredded Monterey Jack cheese

$^1/_4$ cup (1 ounce) crumbled blue cheese

$^1/_4$ cup finely minced green onions (white parts only)

1 jar (2 ounces) diced pimento, drained

10 slices bacon, cooked, drained, finely crumbled and divided

$^3/_4$ cup finely chopped pecans, divided

Salt and black pepper to taste

$^1/_4$ cup minced parsley

1 tablespoon poppy seeds

Beat cream cheese and milk on low speed in large bowl until blended. Add cheeses. Blend on medium speed until well combined. Add green onions, pimento, half of bacon and half of pecans. Blend on medium speed until well mixed. Add salt and pepper to taste. Transfer half of mixture to large piece of plastic wrap. Form into ball; wrap tightly. Repeat with remaining mixture. Refrigerate until chilled, at least two hours.

Combine remaining bacon and pecans with parsley and poppy seeds in pie plate or large dinner plate. Remove plastic wrap from each ball; roll each in bacon mixture until well coated. Wrap each ball tightly in plastic wrap and refrigerate until ready to use, up to 24 hours.

Makes about 24 servings

Antipasto Crescent Bites

2 ounces cream cheese (do not use reduced-fat or fat-free cream cheese)

1 package (8 ounces) refrigerated crescent roll dough

1 egg plus 1 tablespoon water, beaten

4 strips roasted red pepper, cut into $3 \times 3/4$-inch-long strips

2 large marinated artichoke hearts, cut in half lengthwise to $3/4$-inch width

1 thin slice Genoa or other salami, cut into 4 strips

4 small stuffed green olives, cut into halves

1. Preheat oven to 375°F. Cut cream cheese into 16 equal pieces, about 1 teaspoon per piece; set aside.

2. Remove dough from package. Unroll on lightly floured surface. Cut each triangle of dough in half to form 2 triangles. Brush outer edges of triangle lightly with egg mixture.

3. Wrap 1 pepper strip around 1 piece of cream cheese. Place on dough triangle. Fold over and pinch edges to seal; repeat with remaining pepper strips. Place 1 piece artichoke heart and 1 piece of cream cheese on dough triangle. Fold over and pinch edges to seal; repeat with remaining pieces of artichoke hearts. Wrap 1 strip salami around 1 piece of cream cheese. Place on dough triangle. Fold over and pinch edges to seal; repeat with remaining salami. Place 2 olive halves and 1 piece of cream cheese on dough triangle. Fold over and pinch edges to seal; repeat with remaining olives. Place on ungreased baking sheet. Brush with egg mixture.

4. Bake 12 to 14 minutes or until golden brown. Cool on wire rack. Store in airtight container in refrigerator. Reheat on baking sheet in preheated 325°F oven 7 to 8 minutes or until warmed through. Do not microwave.

Makes 16 pieces

Antipasto Crescent Bites

Pesto Cheese Wreath

    Parsley-Basil Pesto* (recipe follows)
 3 packages (8 ounces each) cream cheese, softened
 1/2 cup mayonnaise
 1/4 cup whipping cream or half-and-half
 1 teaspoon sugar
 1 teaspoon onion salt
 1/3 cup chopped roasted red peppers** or pimiento, drained
    Pimiento strips and Italian flat leaf parsley leaves (optional)
    Assorted crackers and cut-up vegetables

*One-half cup purchased pesto may be substituted for Parsley-Basil Pesto.

**Look for roasted red peppers packed in cans or jars in the Italian food section of the supermarket.

Prepare Parsley-Basil Pesto; set aside. Beat cream cheese and mayonnaise in medium bowl until smooth; beat in cream, sugar and onion salt.

Line 5-cup ring mold with plastic wrap. Spoon half of cheese mixture into prepared mold; spread evenly. Spread Parsley-Basil Pesto evenly over cheese mixture; top with chopped red peppers. Spoon remaining cheese mixture over peppers; spread evenly. Cover; refrigerate until cheese mixture is firm, 8 hours or overnight.

Uncover mold; invert onto serving plate. Carefully remove plastic wrap. Smooth top and sides of wreath with spatula. Garnish with pimiento strips and parsley leaves, if desired. Serve with assorted crackers and vegetables.

Makes 16 to 24 appetizer servings

Parsley-Basil Pesto

    2 cups fresh parsley leaves
 1/4 cup pine nuts or slivered almonds
    2 tablespoons grated Parmesan cheese
    2 cloves garlic, peeled
    1 tablespoon dried basil leaves, crushed
 1/4 teaspoon salt
    2 tablespoons olive or vegetable oil

Process all ingredients except oil in food processor or blender until finely
chopped. With machine running, add oil gradually, processing until
mixture is smooth.   *Makes about 1/2 cup*

Pesto Cheese Wreath

Holiday Meat and Vegetable Kabobs

1 cup fresh pearl onions

$^1/_3$ cup olive oil

2 tablespoons balsamic vinegar

1 tablespoon TABASCO® brand Pepper Sauce

1 tablespoon dried basil leaves

2 large cloves garlic, crushed

1 teaspoon salt

1 pound boneless skinless chicken breasts

1 pound boneless beef sirloin

2 large red peppers, cored, seeded and cut into $^3/_4$-inch pieces

1 large green pepper, cored, seeded and cut into $^3/_4$-inch pieces

1 large zucchini, cut into $^3/_4$-inch pieces

Soak 3 dozen 4-inch-long wooden skewers in water overnight. Bring pearl onions and enough water to cover in 1-quart saucepan over high heat to a boil. Reduce heat to low. Cover and simmer 3 minutes or until onions are tender. Drain. When cool enough to handle, peel away outer layer of skin from onions.

Combine oil, vinegar, TABASCO® Sauce, basil, garlic and salt in medium bowl. Pour half of mixture into another bowl. Cut chicken and beef into $^3/_4$-inch pieces and place in bowl with TABASCO® Sauce mixture, tossing well to coat. In remaining bowl of TABASCO® Sauce mixture, toss pearl onions, red and green peppers and zucchini. Let stand at least 30 minutes, tossing occasionally.

Preheat broiler. Skewer 1 piece of chicken or beef and 1 piece each of red pepper, green pepper, onion and zucchini onto each wooden skewer. Broil 4 to 6 minutes, turning occasionally.   *Makes 3 dozen hors d'oeuvres*

Orange Maple Sausage Balls

1 pound BOB EVANS® Original Recipe Roll Sausage

1 small onion, finely chopped

1 small red or yellow bell pepper, finely chopped

1 egg

2 tablespoons uncooked cream of wheat cereal

$\frac{1}{2}$ cup maple syrup or maple-flavored syrup

3 to 5 tablespoons frozen orange juice concentrate, slightly thawed, to taste

Combine first 5 ingredients in large bowl until well blended. Shape into $\frac{3}{4}$-inch balls. Cook in large skillet over medium-high heat until browned on all sides and no longer pink in centers. Drain off drippings. Add syrup and orange juice concentrate to sausage mixture. Cook and stir over medium heat 2 to 3 minutes or until thick bubbly syrup forms. Serve hot. Refrigerate leftovers.   *Makes about 24 appetizers*

Serving Suggestion: Serve on party picks with sautéed mushrooms and water chestnuts. These meatballs would also make an excellent breakfast item; serve with small pancakes.

Cheesy Christmas Trees

$^1/_2$ cup mayonnaise

1 tablespoon dry ranch-style salad dressing mix

1 cup shredded Cheddar cheese

$^1/_4$ cup grated Parmesan cheese

12 slices firm white bread

$^1/_4$ cup red bell pepper strips

$^1/_4$ cup green bell pepper strips

1. Preheat broiler. Combine mayonnaise and salad dressing mix in medium bowl. Add cheeses; mix well.

2. Cut bread slices into Christmas tree shapes using large cookie cutters. Spread each tree with about 1 tablespoon mayonnaise mixture. Decorate with red and green bell pepper strips. Place on baking sheet.

3. Broil 4 inches from heat 2 to 3 minutes or until bubbling. Serve warm.

Makes about 12 appetizers

Running short on time? Simply chop the red and green bell peppers and stir into the cheese mixture. Spread over slices of French bread and broil.

Cheesy Christmas Trees

Holiday Star

TOPPING

3/4 cup sour cream

1/2 cup mayonnaise

2 tablespoons heavy cream

1 teaspoon balsamic vinegar

1/4 cup chopped fresh cilantro

1/4 cup chopped fresh basil

1/4 cup chopped roasted red peppers, drained and patted dry

1/2 teaspoon garlic powder

1/4 teaspoon salt

Black pepper to taste

STAR

2 cans (8 ounces each) refrigerated crescent roll dough

GARNISHES

Red bell pepper, chopped

Green onion, chopped

Black olive slices (optional)

1. Preheat oven to 375°F. Combine sour cream, mayonnaise, heavy cream and balsamic vinegar in medium bowl. Stir in cilantro, basil and roasted red pepper. Add garlic powder, salt and black pepper; mix well. Cover and refrigerate 1 hour or until ready to spread.

2. Place 2-inch round cookie cutter or similar size custard cup in center of 14-inch pizza pan; set aside. Remove dough from first can and unroll on cookie sheet. Seal perforations by pressing down slightly with fingers. Cut 24 circles with 1 1/2-inch cookie cutter. Remove excess dough from cut circles; set aside. Repeat with second can.

3. Evenly space five dough circles around the outside edge of the pizza pan. (These will be the star points.) From each star point, make a triangle pattern with rows of slightly overlapping dough circles, working toward the cookie cutter in center of pan. Roll excess dough into a ball; flatten with hands. Cut more circles as needed to completely fill star.

4. Remove cookie cutter in center of star. Bake 12 to 16 minutes or until light golden brown. Cool completely, in pan on wire rack, about 30 minutes.

5. Spread topping over star. Garnish with red bell pepper, green onion and black olives, if desired. Place decorative candle in center of star. Serve immediately.   *Makes about 16 servings*

Holiday Star

Yuletide Soups & Salads

Complement your holiday meal with delicious accompaniments of colorful salads and creamy soups.

Potato and Leek Soup

    4 cups chicken broth

    3 potatoes, peeled and diced

1 1/2 cups chopped cabbage

    1 leek, diced

    1 onion, chopped

    2 carrots, diced

    1/4 cup chopped fresh parsley

    1 teaspoon salt

    1/2 teaspoon black pepper

    1/2 teaspoon caraway seeds

    1 bay leaf

    1/2 cup sour cream

    1 pound bacon, cooked and crumbled

Slow Cooker Directions

Combine chicken broth, potatoes, cabbage, leek, onion, carrots and parsley in large bowl; pour mixture into slow cooker. Stir in salt, pepper, caraway seeds and bay leaf. Cover and cook on Low 8 to 10 hours or on High 4 to 5 hours. Remove and discard bay leaf. Combine some hot liquid from slow cooker with sour cream in small bowl. Add mixture to slow cooker; stir. Stir in bacon.   *Makes 6 to 8 servings*

Winter Pear and Stilton Salad

$^{1}/_{3}$ cup extra virgin olive oil

$1^{1}/_{2}$ tablespoons sherry wine vinegar or white wine vinegar

4 teaspoons honey

1 tablespoon Dijon mustard

$^{1}/_{4}$ teaspoon salt

2 ripe Bosc, Bartlett or Anjou pears

Lemon juice

5 cups assorted gourmet mixed salad greens (such as oakleaf, frisee, watercress, radicchio, arugula or escarole), torn into bite size pieces

2 cups torn Boston or Bibb lettuce leaves

$1^{1}/_{2}$ cups (6 ounces) Stilton or Gorgonzola cheese, crumbled

Black pepper

Place oil, vinegar, honey, mustard and salt in small bowl. Whisk together until combined. Cover and refrigerate up to 2 days.

Cut pears into quarters; remove stem and core. Cut each quarter into $^{1}/_{2}$-inch pieces. To help prevent discoloration, brush pear pieces with lemon juice, if desired.

Combine all salad greens in large bowl. Add pears, cheese and dressing. Toss lightly to coat; sprinkle with pepper.   *Makes 6 to 8 servings*

Winter Pear and Stilton Salad

Cajun Christmas Gumbo

10 to 12 chicken thighs (4 to 5 pounds)

$^1/_4$ cup olive or vegetable oil

1 cup chopped onion

$^1/_2$ cup chopped green bell pepper

$^1/_3$ cup all-purpose flour

2 cloves garlic, crushed

1 can (28 ounces) whole peeled tomatoes

2 cups chicken broth or water

$^1/_2$ teaspoon crushed red pepper flakes

$^1/_2$ teaspoon dried thyme leaves, crushed

1 bay leaf

$^1/_2$ package (10 ounces) frozen sliced okra

24 ounces surimi seafood, crab flavored, chunk or flake style

$^1/_2$ pint standard oysters

$^1/_2$ cup fresh parsley, finely chopped

Hot cooked white rice

Preheat oven to 350°F. Place chicken thighs in single layer in shallow baking pan. Bake 45 to 50 minutes or until chicken is no longer pink and juices run clear.

Meanwhile, heat oil in Dutch oven. Add onion and bell pepper; cook over medium-low heat 10 minutes or until onion is translucent, stirring occasionally. Stir in flour; reduce heat to low. Cook 5 minutes, stirring occasionally. Add garlic, tomatoes, chicken broth, red pepper, thyme and bay leaf. Cook, uncovered, stirring constantly, until slightly thickened. Cover; cook over low heat 30 minutes, stirring occasionally to prevent sticking.

Add cooked chicken with pan juices and okra to vegetable mixture. Increase heat to medium-low; simmer 15 to 20 minutes. Stir in surimi seafood, oysters and parsley; cook 5 to 10 minutes until seafood is heated through and oysters begin to curl. Remove and discard bay leaf. Pour gumbo into soup tureen or serving bowl. Ladle gumbo over rice in soup bowls to serve.   *Makes 10 to 12 servings*

Favorite recipe from **National Fisheries Institute**

Holiday Fruit Salad

> 3 packages (3 ounces each) strawberry flavor gelatin
> 3 cups boiling water
> 2 ripe DOLE® Bananas
> 1 package (16 ounces) frozen strawberries
> 1 can (20 ounces) DOLE® Crushed Pineapple
> 1 package (8 ounces) cream cheese, softened
> 1 cup dairy sour cream or plain yogurt
> 1/4 cup sugar
>   Crisp DOLE® Lettuce leaves

• In large bowl, dissolve gelatin in boiling water. Slice bananas into gelatin mixture. Add frozen strawberries and undrained pineapple. Reserve half of the mixture at room temperature. Pour remaining mixture into 13×9-inch pan. Refrigerate 1 hour or until firm.

• In mixer bowl, beat cream cheese with sour cream and sugar; spread over chilled layer. Gently spoon reserved gelatin mixture on top. Refrigerate until firm, about 2 hours. Cut into squares; serve on lettuce-lined salad plates. Garnish with additional pineapple and mint leaves, until firm.

Makes 12 servings

Spicy Pumpkin Soup with Green Chili Swirl

1 can (4 ounces) diced green chilies

1/4 cup reduced-fat sour cream

1/4 cup fresh cilantro leaves

1 can (15 ounces) solid-pack pumpkin

1 can (about 14 ounces) fat-free reduced-sodium chicken broth

1/2 cup water

1 teaspoon ground cumin

1/2 teaspoon chili powder

1/4 teaspoon garlic powder

1/8 teaspoon ground red pepper (optional)

1. Combine green chilies, sour cream and cilantro in food processor or blender; process until smooth.*

2. Combine pumpkin, chicken broth, water, cumin, chili powder, garlic powder and pepper, if desired, in medium saucepan; stir in 1/4 cup green chili mixture. Bring to a boil; reduce heat to medium. Simmer, uncovered 5 minutes, stirring occasionally.

3. Pour into serving bowls. Top each serving with a small dollop of remaining green chili mixture. Run tip of spoon through dollop to swirl.

Makes 4 servings

Omit food processor step by adding green chilies directly to soup. Finely chop cilantro and combine with sour cream. Dollop with sour cream-cilantro mixture as directed.

Spicy Pumpkin Soup with Green Chili Swirl

Christmas Ribbon

2 packages (4-serving size each) or 1 package (8-serving size)
JELL-O® Brand Strawberry Flavor Gelatin Dessert
5 cups boiling water, divided
2/3 cup BREAKSTONE'S® or KNUDSEN® Sour Cream or
BREYERS® Plain or Vanilla Lowfat Yogurt, divided
2 packages (4-serving size each) or 1 package (8-serving size)
JELL-O® Brand Lime Flavor Gelatin Dessert

Dissolve strawberry flavor gelatin in $2\frac{1}{2}$ cups of the boiling water. Pour $1\frac{1}{2}$ cups gelatin into 6-cup ring mold. Chill until set but not firm, about 30 minutes. Chill remaining gelatin in bowl until slightly thickened; gradually blend in $1/3$ cup of the sour cream. Spoon over gelatin in mold. Chill until set but not firm, about 15 minutes.

Repeat with lime flavor gelatin, using remaining $2\frac{1}{2}$ cups boiling water and $1/3$ cup sour cream. Chill dissolved gelatin before measuring and pouring into mold. Chill at least 2 hours. Unmold. *Makes 12 servings*

Prep Time: 30 minutes
Chill Time: 3 hours

Choose the best container for efficiency when making this recipe. Metal bowls chill more quickly than glass or plastic bowls so your gelatin will be firm in less time.

Christmas Ribbon

Mixed Greens with Raspberry Vinaigrette

$^1/_2$ cup walnut halves

$^1/_3$ cup vegetable oil

$2^1/_2$ tablespoons raspberry vinegar

1 tablespoon chopped shallot

$^1/_2$ teaspoon salt

$^1/_2$ teaspoon sugar

2 cups washed and torn Romaine lettuce leaves

2 cups washed and torn spinach leaves

2 cups washed and torn red leaf lettuce leaves

1 cup halved red seedless grapes

Preheat oven to 350°F. To toast walnuts, spread in single layer on baking sheet. Bake 6 to 8 minutes or until lightly golden brown, stirring frequently; cool. Coarsely chop; set aside.

Place oil, vinegar, shallot, salt and sugar in small bowl or small jar with lid. Whisk together or cover and shake jar until mixed. Cover; refrigerate up to 1 week. Combine greens, grapes and chopped walnuts in large bowl. Just before serving, add dressing; toss well to coat.

Makes 6 to 8 servings

Mixed Greens with Raspberry Vinaigrette

Creamy Clam Chowder

2¹/₂ cups water, divided

20 fresh hard-shell clams,* scrubbed and soaked

2 strips thick-sliced bacon

1 medium onion, chopped

1 rib celery, diced

4 tablespoons all-purpose flour

1 clove garlic, minced

3 medium red potatoes, peeled and diced

2 bay leaves

1 teaspoon salt

¹/₈ teaspoon black pepper

2 cups half-and-half

1 cup milk

Oyster crackers and lemon slices for garnish

*If fresh clams in shells are not available, substitute ³/₄ to 1 cup shucked clams. Omit step 1.

1. Place 1 cup water in large stockpot. Bring to a boil over high heat. Add clams. Cover stockpot; reduce heat to medium. Steam 5 to 7 minutes or until clams start to open. Remove clams from stockpot as they open. Discard any clams that remain unopened.

2. Remove clams from shells. Chop clams; set aside. (For shucked clams, drain and chop clams; set aside.)

3. Cook bacon in large saucepan over medium-high heat until crisp. Remove bacon to paper towels, leaving drippings in pan. Crumble bacon when cool enough to handle.

4. Add onion, celery, flour and garlic to bacon drippings and cook over medium heat, stirring occasionally, about 2 minutes or until vegetables are crisp-tender. Remove from heat.

5. Add potatoes to onion mixture. Stir in remaining $1\frac{1}{2}$ cups water, bay leaves, salt and pepper. Bring to a boil over high heat. Reduce heat to medium-low; simmer, uncovered, until potatoes are tender, about 10 minutes.

6. Stir in half-and-half, milk and chopped clams; heat through over medium heat, stirring occasionally. Discard bay leaves. Stir in bacon. Serve with oyster crackers, if desired.   *Makes 6 servings*

Creamy Clam Chowder

Pear and Cranberry Salad

$^{1}/_{2}$ cup canned whole berry cranberry sauce

2 tablespoons balsamic vinegar

1 tablespoon olive or canola oil

12 cups (9 ounces) packed assorted bitter or gourmet salad greens

6 small or 4 large pears (about 1 $^{3}/_{4}$ pounds)

2 ounces blue or Gorgonzola cheese, crumbled

Black pepper

1. Combine cranberry sauce, vinegar and oil in small bowl; mix well. (Dressing may be covered and refrigerated up to 2 days before serving.)

2. Arrange greens on six serving plates. Cut pears lengthwise into $^{1}/_{2}$-inch-thick slices; cut core and seeds from each slice. Arrange pears attractively over greens. Drizzle cranberry dressing over pears and greens; sprinkle with cheese. Sprinkle with pepper to taste.   *Makes 6 servings*

Prep Time: 20 minutes

Be sure to use ripe pears. Forelles and
Red Bartletts are particularly well suited
for use in this salad.

Pear and Cranberry Salad

Double Corn & Cheddar Chowder

1 tablespoon margarine

1 cup chopped onion

2 tablespoons all-purpose flour

2½ cups fat-free reduced-sodium chicken broth

1 can (16 ounces) cream-style corn

1 cup frozen whole kernel corn

½ cup finely diced red bell pepper

½ teaspoon hot pepper sauce

¾ cup (3 ounces) shredded sharp Cheddar cheese

Black pepper (optional)

1. Melt margarine in large saucepan over medium heat. Add onion; cook and stir 5 minutes. Sprinkle onion with flour; cook and stir 1 minute.

2. Add chicken broth; bring to a boil, stirring frequently. Add cream-style corn, corn kernels, bell pepper and pepper sauce; bring to a simmer. Cover; simmer 15 minutes.

3. Remove from heat; gradually stir in cheese until melted. Ladle into soup bowls; sprinkle with black pepper, if desired.   *Makes 6 servings*

Double Corn & Cheddar Chowder

Merry Main Dishes

*Choose from the many truly classic
recipes for a magnificent main course to
highlight memorable holiday feasts.*

Herb Roasted Turkey

1 (12-pound) turkey, thawed if frozen
$^1/_2$ cup FLEISCHMANN'S® Original Margarine, softened, divided
1 tablespoon Italian seasoning

1. Remove neck and giblets from turkey cavities. Rinse turkey; drain well and pat dry. Free legs from tucked position; do not cut band of skin. Using rubber spatula or hand, loosen skin over breast, starting at body cavity opening by legs.

2. Blend 6 tablespoons margarine and Italian seasoning. Spread 2 tablespoons herb mixture inside body cavity; spread remaining herb mixture on meat under skin. Hold skin in place at opening with wooden picks. Return legs to tucked position; turn wings back to hold neck skin in place.

3. Place turkey, breast-side up, on flat rack in shallow open pan. Insert meat thermometer deep into thickest part of thigh next to body, not touching bone. Melt remaining 2 tablespoons margarine; brush over skin.

4. Roast at 325°F for 3$^1/_2$ to 3$^3/_4$ hours. When skin is golden brown, shield breast loosely with foil to prevent overbrowning. Check for doneness; thigh temperature should be 180 to 185°F. Transfer turkey to cutting board; let stand 15 to 20 minutes before carving. Remove wooden toothpicks just before carving.   *Makes 12 servings*

Preparation Time: 20 minutes
Cook Time: 3 hours and 30 minutes
Cooling Time: 15 minutes
Total Time: 4 hours and 5 minutes

Pork Tenderloin with Grilled Apple Cream Sauce

1 can (6 ounces) frozen apple juice concentrate, thawed and divided (³/₄ cup)

¹/₂ cup Calvados or brandy, divided

2 tablespoons Dijon mustard

1 tablespoon olive oil

3 cloves garlic, minced

1¹/₄ teaspoons salt, divided

¹/₄ teaspoon black pepper

1¹/₂ pounds pork tenderloin

2 green or red apples, cored

1 tablespoon butter

¹/₂ large red onion, cut into thin slivers

¹/₂ cup heavy cream

Fresh thyme sprigs

Reserve 2 tablespoons juice concentrate. Combine remaining juice concentrate, ¹/₄ cup Calvados, mustard, oil, garlic, 1 teaspoon salt and pepper in glass dish. Add pork; turn to coat. Cover and refrigerate 2 hours, turning pork occasionally. Cut apples crosswise into ³/₈-inch rings. Remove pork from marinade; discard marinade. Grill pork on covered grill over medium KINGSFORD® Briquets about 20 minutes, turning 3 times, until meat thermometer inserted in thickest part registers 155°F. Grill apples about 4 minutes per side until tender; cut rings into quarters. Melt butter in large skillet over medium heat. Add onion; cook and stir until soft. Stir in apples, remaining ¹/₄ cup Calvados, ¹/₄ teaspoon salt and reserved 2 tablespoons juice concentrate. Add cream; heat through. Cut pork crosswise into ¹/₂-inch slices; spoon sauce over pork. Garnish with fresh thyme. *Makes 4 servings*

Pork Tenderloin with Grilled Apple Cream Sauce

Baked Holiday Ham with Cranberry-Wine Compote

2 teaspoons peanut oil

$^2/_3$ cup chopped onion

$^1/_2$ cup chopped celery

1 cup red wine

1 cup honey

$^1/_2$ cup sugar

1 package (12 ounces) fresh cranberries

1 fully-cooked smoked ham (10 pounds)

Whole cloves

Kumquats and currant leaves for garnish

1. For Cranberry-Wine Compote, heat oil in large saucepan over medium-high heat until hot; add onion and celery. Cook until tender, stirring frequently. Stir in wine, honey and sugar; bring to a boil. Add cranberries; return to a boil. Reduce heat to low; cover and simmer 10 minutes. Cool completely.

2. Carefully ladle enough clear syrup from cranberry mixture into glass measuring cup to equal 1 cup; set aside. Transfer remaining cranberry mixture to small serving bowl; cover and refrigerate.

3. Slice away skin from ham with sharp utility knife. (Omit step if meat retailer has already removed skin.)

4. Preheat oven to 325°F. Score fat on ham in diamond design with sharp utility knife; stud with whole cloves. Place ham, fat side up, on rack in shallow roasting pan.

5. Bake, uncovered, 1½ hours. Baste ham with reserved cranberry-wine syrup. Bake 1 to 2 hours more or until meat thermometer inserted into thickest part of ham, not touching bone, registers 140°F, basting with cranberry-wine syrup twice. Let ham stand 10 minutes. Serve warm with chilled Cranberry-Wine Compote. Garnish, if desired.

Makes 16 to 20 servings

Baked Holiday Ham with Cranberry-Wine Compote

Beef Tenderloin with Roasted Vegetables

1 beef tenderloin (3 pounds), well trimmed
1/2 cup chardonnay or other dry white wine
1/2 cup reduced-sodium soy sauce
2 cloves garlic, sliced
1 tablespoon fresh rosemary
1 tablespoon Dijon mustard
1 teaspoon dry mustard
1 pound small red or white potatoes, cut into 1-inch pieces
1 pound brussels sprouts
12 ounces baby carrots

1. Place tenderloin in resealable plastic food storage bag. Combine wine, soy sauce, garlic, rosemary, Dijon mustard and dry mustard in small bowl. Pour over tenderloin. Seal bag; turn bag to coat. Marinate in refrigerator 4 to 12 hours, turning several times.

2. Preheat oven to 425°F. Spray 13×9-inch baking pan with nonstick cooking spray. Place potatoes, brussels sprouts and carrots in pan. Remove tenderloin from marinade. Pour marinade over vegetables; toss to coat well. Cover vegetables with foil. Bake 30 minutes; stir. Place tenderloin on vegetables. Bake 45 minutes for medium or until internal temperature reaches 145°F when tested with meat thermometer inserted into the thickest part of roast. Transfer roast to cutting board; cover with foil. Let stand 10 to 15 minutes before carving. Internal temperature will continue to rise 5°F to 10°F during stand time.

3. Stir vegetables; test for doneness and continue to bake if not tender. Slice tenderloin; arrange on serving platter with roasted vegetables. Garnish with fresh rosemary, if desired. *Makes 10 servings*

Beef Tenderloin with Roasted Vegetables

Roast Turkey with Fresh Herb Stuffing

4 cups cubed fresh herb- or garlic-flavored breadsticks
1 turkey (8 to 10 pounds)
1 tablespoon margarine
1 1/2 cups sliced brown mushrooms
1 cup chopped onion
2/3 cup chopped celery
1/4 cup chopped fresh parsley
2 tablespoons chopped fresh tarragon
1 tablespoon chopped fresh thyme
1/4 teaspoon black pepper
1/4 cup reduced-sodium chicken broth

1. Preheat oven to 350°F. Place cubed breadsticks on nonstick baking sheet. Bake 20 minutes to dry.

2. Remove giblets from turkey. Rinse turkey and cavities; pat dry with paper towels. Melt margarine in large nonstick skillet. Add mushrooms, onion and celery. Cook and stir 5 minutes or until onion is soft and golden; remove from heat. Add parsley, tarragon, thyme, pepper and bread cubes; stir until blended. Gently mix chicken broth into bread cube mixture. Fill turkey cavities with stuffing.

3. Spray roasting pan with nonstick cooking spray. Place turkey, breast side up, in roasting pan. Bake in 350°F oven 3 hours or until meat thermometer inserted in thigh registers 180°F and juices run clear.

4. Transfer turkey to serving platter. Cover loosely with foil; let stand 20 minutes. Remove and discard skin. Slice turkey and serve with herb stuffing.   *Makes 10 servings*

Holiday Pork Roast

1 tablespoon minced fresh ginger

2 cloves garlic, minced

1 teaspoon dried sage leaves, crushed

$^1/_4$ teaspoon salt

1 (5- to 7-pound) pork loin roast

$^1/_3$ cup apple jelly

$^1/_2$ teaspoon TABASCO® brand Pepper Sauce

2 medium carrots, sliced

2 medium onions, sliced

1$^3/_4$ cups water, divided

1 teaspoon browning and seasoning sauce

Preheat oven to 325°F. Combine ginger, garlic, sage and salt; rub over pork. Place in shallow roasting pan. Roast pork 1$^1/_2$ hours. Remove from oven; score meat in diamond pattern.

Combine jelly and TABASCO® Sauce; spread generously over roast. Arrange carrots and onions around meat; add 1 cup water. Roast 1 hour until meat thermometer registers 170°F. Remove roast to serving platter; keep warm.

Skim fat from drippings in pan; discard fat. Place vegetables and drippings in food processor or blender; process until puréed. Return purée to roasting pan. Stir in remaining $^3/_4$ cup water and browning sauce; heat. Serve sauce with roast.   *Makes 6 to 8 servings*

Roasted Herb & Garlic Tenderloin

1 well-trimmed beef tenderloin roast (3 to 4 pounds)
1 tablespoon black peppercorns
2 tablespoons chopped fresh basil *or* 2 teaspoons dried basil leaves
4¹/₂ teaspoons chopped fresh thyme *or* 1¹/₂ teaspoons dried thyme
    leaves
1 tablespoon chopped fresh rosemary *or* 1 teaspoon dried
    rosemary
1 tablespoon minced garlic
    Salt and black pepper (optional)

1. Preheat oven to 425°F. To hold shape of roast, tie roast with cotton string in 1¹/₂-inch intervals.

2. Place peppercorns in small heavy resealable plastic food storage bag. Squeeze out excess air; seal bag tightly. Pound peppercorns with flat side of meat mallet or rolling pin until peppercorns are cracked.

3. Place roast on meat rack in shallow roasting pan. Combine cracked peppercorns, basil, thyme, rosemary and garlic in small bowl; rub over top surface of roast.

4. Roast in oven 40 to 50 minutes for medium or until internal temperatures reaches 145°F when tested with meat thermometer inserted into the thickest part of roast.

5. Transfer roast to cutting board; cover with foil. Let stand 10 to 15 minutes before carving. Internal temperature will continue to rise 5°F to 10°F during stand time. Remove and discard string. To serve, carve crosswise into ¹/₂-inch-thick slices with large carving knife. Season with salt and pepper. *Makes 10 to 12 servings*

Roasted Herb & Garlic Tenderloin

Crown Roast of Pork with Peach Stuffing

    1 (7- to 8-pound) crown roast of pork (12 to 16 ribs)
1 ^{1}/$_2$ cups water
    1 cup FLEISCHMANN'S® Original Margarine, divided
    1 (15-ounce) package seasoned bread cubes
    1 cup chopped celery
    2 medium onions, chopped
    1 (16-ounce) can sliced peaches, drained and chopped, reserve
       liquid
  ^{1}/$_2$ cup seedless raisins

1. Place crown roast, bone tips up, on rack in shallow roasting pan. Make a ball of foil and press into cavity to hold open. Wrap bone tips in foil. Roast at 325°F, uncovered, for 2 hours; baste with pan drippings occasionally.

2. Heat water and ^{3}/$_4$ cup margarine in large heavy pot to a boil; remove from heat. Add bread cubes, tossing lightly with a fork; set aside.

3. Cook and stir celery and onions in remaining margarine in large skillet over medium-high heat until tender, about 5 minutes.

4. Add celery mixture, peaches with liquid and raisins to bread cube mixture, tossing to mix well.

5. Remove foil from center of roast. Spoon stuffing lightly into cavity. Roast 30 to 45 minutes more or until meat thermometer registers 155°F (internal temperature will rise to 160°F upon standing).

Cover stuffing with foil, if necessary, to prevent overbrowning. Bake any remaining stuffing in greased, covered casserole during last 30 minutes of roasting. *Makes 12 to 16 servings*

Preparation Time: 45 minutes
Cook Time: 2 hours and 30 minutes
Total Time: 3 hours and 15 minutes

Crown Roast of Pork with Peach Stuffing

Stuffed Cornish Hens for Christmas

4 PERDUE® Fresh Cornish Game Hens

1 tablespoon butter or margarine

1 tablespoon prepared mustard, preferably Pommery

   Corn oil for frying

2 medium potatoes, peeled and cut into $^1/_2$-inch cubes

$^1/_2$ pound (1 large) chayote, peeled and cut into $^1/_2$-inch cubes *or*

      3 to 4 carrots, cut into $^1/_2$-inch cubes

$^1/_2$ cup chopped onion

2 cloves garlic, chopped

   Livers from Cornish Hens, sliced

$^1/_2$ cup coarsely chopped red or green bell pepper

$^1/_4$ cup chopped ripe tomato

1 tablespoon raisins

1 teaspoon salt or to taste

$^1/_4$ teaspoon black pepper

12 stuffed green olives

1 tablespoon cider vinegar

1 teaspoon dried thyme leaves, crushed

$^1/_2$ cup red wine

Remove giblets from hens (reserving livers). Rinse hens; pat dry with paper towel. Rub inside and out with mixture of butter and mustard. In heavy skillet, heat 1 tablespoon oil over medium heat. Brown hens lightly and remove.

In small saucepan, cook potatoes and chayote in boiling water for 5 minutes. Pour off water and drain vegetables on paper towels.

Heat 2 tablespoons oil in skillet. Add potatoes, chayote, onion, garlic, livers, bell pepper, tomato, raisins, salt, black pepper and olives. Stir-fry 5 minutes over moderate heat, adding vinegar during last minute.

Preheat oven to 350°F. Stuff hens firmly with potato mixture, folding skin over cavity or closing with skewer. Place hens in large roasting pan, breast side up. Surround with remaining potato mixture; sprinkle hens with thyme and pour wine over all. Roast, uncovered, about 1 hour or until a meat thermometer inserted in thigh registers 180°F and juices run clear when thigh is pierced, basting occasionally.   *Makes 4 servings*

Prime Ribs of Beef à la Lawry's®

1 (8-pound) prime rib roast
LAWRY'S® Seasoned Salt
Rock Salt

Preheat oven to 500°F.

Score fat on meat and rub generously with Seasoned Salt. Cover bottom of roasting pan with rock salt 1 inch deep. Place roast directly on rock salt and bake, uncovered, 8 minutes per pound for rare.   *Makes 8 servings*

Serving Suggestion: Garnish with watercress and spiced crab apples. Carve at tableside. Serve with additional Seasoned Salt.

Fruited Pork Loin

1 cup dried apricot halves

$^1/_2$ cup dry sherry

1 (3- to 5-pound) center cut pork rib or loin roast, backbone
  cracked

1 cup KARO® Light or Dark Corn Syrup

1 tablespoon grated orange peel

$^1/_2$ cup orange juice

$^1/_4$ cup soy sauce

1. In small saucepan, combine apricots and sherry. Cover and cook over medium heat, stirring occasionally, until liquid is absorbed.

2. Trim excess fat from surface of roast. Cut deep slits in meat directly over rib bones; insert 3 or 4 apricots in each slit. Place roast, bone-side down, on rack in roasting pan.

3. Roast in 325°F oven 1 to 2 hours* or until meat thermometer registers 160°F.

4. Meanwhile, prepare glaze. In small saucepan, stir corn syrup, orange peel, orange juice and soy sauce. Bring to boil; reduce heat and simmer 5 minutes. Set aside half of glaze to serve with pork loin.

5. Brush pork loin frequently with remaining glaze during last 30 minutes of roasting. Serve with reserved glaze. *Makes 6 to 10 servings*

Roast pork loin at 325°F for 20 to 25 minutes per pound.

Prep Time: 20 minutes
Bake Time: 1 to 2 hours

Fruited Pork Loin

Lemon-Garlic Roasted Chicken

    1 chicken (3^1/$_2$ to 4 pounds)
      Salt and black pepper
    2 tablespoons butter or margarine, softened
    2 lemons, cut into halves
    4 to 6 cloves garlic, peeled and left whole
    5 to 6 sprigs fresh rosemary
      Garlic Sauce (recipe follows)
      Additional rosemary sprigs and lemon wedges

Rinse chicken; pat dry with paper towels. Season with salt and pepper, then rub skin with butter. Place lemons, garlic and rosemary in cavity of chicken. Tuck wings under back and tie legs together with cotton string.

Arrange medium-low KINGSFORD® Briquets on each side of rectangular metal or foil drip pan. Pour in hot tap water to fill pan half full. Place chicken, breast side up, on grid, directly above drip pan. Grill chicken, on covered grill, about 1 hour or until meat thermometer inserted in thigh registers 175° to 180°F or until joints move easily and juices run clear when chicken is pierced. Add few briquets to both sides of fire, if necessary, to maintain constant temperature.

While chicken is cooking, prepare Garlic Sauce. When chicken is done, carefully lift from grill to wide shallow bowl so that juices from cavity run into bowl. Transfer juices to small saucepan; bring to a boil. Boil juices 2 minutes; transfer to small bowl or gravy boat. Carve chicken; serve with Garlic Sauce and cooking juices. Garnish with rosemary sprigs and lemon wedges. *Makes 4 servings*

Garlic Sauce

    2 tablespoons olive oil

    1 large head of garlic, cloves separated and peeled

    2 (1-inch-wide) strips lemon peel

    1 can (14$\frac{1}{2}$ ounces) low-salt chicken broth

$\frac{1}{2}$ cup water

    1 sprig *each* sage and oregano *or* 2 to 3 sprigs parsley

$\frac{1}{4}$ cup butter, softened

Heat oil in a saucepan; add garlic cloves and lemon peel. Sauté over medium-low heat, stirring frequently, until garlic just starts to brown in a few spots. Add broth, water and herbs; simmer to reduce mixture by about half. Discard herb sprigs and lemon peel. Transfer broth mixture to a blender or food processor; process until smooth. Return garlic purée to the saucepan and whisk in butter over very low heat until smooth. Sauce can be rewarmed before serving.   *Makes about 1 cup*

Lemon-Garlic Roasted Chicken

Rack of Lamb with Dijon-Mustard Sauce

1 rack of lamb (3 pounds), all visible fat removed
1 cup finely chopped fresh parsley
$^1\!/_2$ cup Dijon mustard
$^1\!/_2$ cup soft whole wheat bread crumbs
1 tablespoon chopped fresh rosemary *or* 2 teaspoons dried
    rosemary
1 teaspoon minced garlic
    Fresh rosemary, lemon slices and lemon peel strips (optional)

Preheat oven to 500°F. Place lamb in large baking pan. Combine parsley, mustard, bread crumbs, rosemary and garlic in small bowl. Spread evenly over top of lamb. Place in center of oven; cook 7 minutes for medium-rare. Turn off oven but do not open door for at least 30 minutes. Serve 2 to 3 chops on each plate, depending on size and total number of chops. Garnish with additional fresh rosemary, lemon slices and lemon peel strips, if desired.

Makes 6 servings

For a beautiful presentation, rub the lamb bones with olive oil before roasting. When the lamb is removed from the oven, the bones will have a nice shine and deep brown color.

Rack of Lamb with Dijon-Mustard Sauce

Santa's Favorite Sides

*Take the mystery out of what side dish
to serve. Choose from fresh vegetables,
hearty potatoes, savory stuffings and
more to make every meal complete.*

Glazed Maple Acorn Squash

1 large acorn or golden acorn squash

$^1/_4$ cup water

2 tablespoons pure maple syrup

1 tablespoon margarine or butter, melted

$^1/_4$ teaspoon ground cinnamon

1. Preheat oven to 375°F.

2. Cut stem and blossom ends from squash. Cut squash crosswise into four equal slices. Discard seeds and membrane. Place water in 13×9-inch baking dish. Arrange squash in dish; cover with foil. Bake 30 minutes or until tender.

3. Combine syrup, margarine and cinnamon in small bowl; mix well. Uncover squash; pour off water. Brush squash with syrup mixture, letting excess pool in center of squash.

4. Return to oven; bake 10 minutes or until syrup mixture is bubbly.

Makes 4 servings

Twice Baked Ranch Potatoes

  4 baking potatoes
  $^1/_2$ cup KRAFT® Ranch Dressing
  $^1/_4$ cup BREAKSTONE'S® or KNUDSEN® Sour Cream
  1 tablespoon OSCAR MAYER® Real Bacon Bits
  $^1/_4$ pound (4 ounces) VELVEETA® Pasteurized Prepared Cheese
      Product, cut up

1. Bake potatoes at 400°F for 1 hour. Slice off tops of potatoes; scoop out centers, leaving $^1/_8$-inch shell.

2. Mash potatoes. Add dressing, sour cream and bacon bits; beat until fluffy. Stir Velveeta into potato mixture. Spoon into shells.

3. Bake at 350°F for 20 minutes.   *Makes 4 servings*

How to Bake Potatoes: Russet potatoes are best for baking. Scrub potatoes well, blot dry and rub the skin with a little oil and salt. Prick the skin of the potatoes with a fork so steam can escape. Stand them on end in a muffin tin. Bake at 400°F for 60 minutes or until tender.

Prep Time: 20 minutes plus baking potatoes
Bake Time: 20 minutes

Always store potatoes in a cool, dark, dry, well-ventilated place. Do not refrigerate them. It is important to protect them from light as it may cause them to turn green and lose quality.

Twice Baked Ranch Potatoes

Corn Pudding Soufflé

2 tablespoons butter or margarine

2 tablespoons all-purpose flour

Half-and-half

1 can (17 ounces) whole kernel corn, drained, liquid reserved

$^1/_4$ cup canned chopped green chilies, drained

Dash garlic powder

2 eggs, separated

$^1/_4$ cup cream-style cottage cheese

Preheat oven to 350°F. Melt butter in medium saucepan over medium heat. Stir in flour until smooth. Add enough half-and-half to corn liquid to measure 1 cup. Gradually stir liquid into saucepan. Continue stirring until sauce is smooth and hot. Stir in corn, chilies and garlic powder.

Bring corn mixture to a boil over medium heat, stirring constantly. Reduce heat to low. Beat egg yolks in small bowl. Stir about $^1/_4$ cup of hot sauce into egg yolks, beating constantly. Stir egg yolk mixture back into sauce. Remove from heat; stir in cottage cheese. Beat egg whites in narrow bowl until stiff peaks form. Fold egg whites into corn mixture. Pour into *ungreased* 1$^1/_2$-quart soufflé dish. Bake 30 minutes or until toothpick inserted in center comes out clean. *Makes 4 to 6 servings*

Broccoli & Red Pepper Sauté

 2 tablespoons olive or vegetable oil

 4 cups small broccoli florets

 1 large red bell pepper, cut into thin strips

 1 medium onion, sliced

 1 clove garlic, finely chopped

 1 envelope LIPTON® Recipe Secrets® Savory Herb with Garlic
     Soup Mix

 ¹/₄ cup sliced almonds, toasted (optional)

In 12-inch skillet, heat oil over medium heat and cook broccoli, bell pepper, onion and garlic 5 minutes or until onion is tender, stirring occasionally. Combine Soup Mix with 1 cup water; add to vegetable mixture. Simmer covered 5 minutes or until broccoli is tender. Sprinkle with almonds.

Makes about 6 servings

Broccoli & Red Pepper Sauté

Fresh Cranberry Relish

1 orange
1 package (12 ounces) fresh or thawed frozen cranberries
2 medium tart apples, unpeeled, cored and coarsely chopped
5¼ teaspoons EQUAL® FOR RECIPES *or* 18 packets EQUAL®
sweetener *or* ¾ cup EQUAL® SPOONFUL™
⅛ teaspoon salt

• Grate rind from orange and reserve. Peel orange; cut orange into large pieces.

• Place orange rind, orange pieces, cranberries and apples in food processor; process until finely chopped. Stir in Equal® and salt. Refrigerate until ready to serve. *Makes 12 servings*

Note: Amount of Equal® may vary depending on the tartness of the apples and cranberries.

Cranberry Gelatin Salad: Prepare 2 packages (0.3 ounce each) sugar-free raspberry gelatin according to package directions using 1½ cups boiling water and 1½ cups cold water; refrigerate until mixture is consistency of unbeaten egg whites. Prepare Fresh Cranberry Relish as directed above; stir into gelatin mixture and spoon into lightly greased 8-cup mold or casserole. Refrigerate until set, about 4 hours. To unmold, briefly dip mold into warm water and loosen top edge of mold with tip of sharp knife. Unmold onto serving plate lined with salad greens. Makes 12 (⅔-cup) servings.

Original Green Bean Casserole

1 can (10³/₄ ounces) condensed cream of mushroom soup

³/₄ cup milk

¹/₈ teaspoon ground black pepper

2 packages (9 ounces each) frozen cut green beans, thawed and
   drained *or* 2 cans (14.5 ounces each) cut green beans,
   drained

1¹/₃ cups *French's*® *Taste Toppers*™ French Fried Onions, divided

Preheat oven to 350°F. Combine soup, milk and ground pepper in
1¹/₂ quart casserole; stir until well blended. Stir in beans and ²/₃ *cup Taste
Toppers*.

Bake, uncovered, 30 minutes or until hot. Stir; sprinkle with remaining
²/₃ *cup Taste Toppers*. Bake 5 minutes or until *Taste Toppers* are golden.

Makes 6 servings

MICROWAVE DIRECTIONS: Prepare green bean mixture as above;
pour into 1¹/₂-quart microwave-safe casserole. Cook, covered, on HIGH
8 to 10 minutes or until heated through. Stir beans halfway through
cooking time. Top with remaining *Taste Toppers*; cook, uncovered,
1 minute. Let stand 5 minutes.

Prep Time: 5 minutes

Sweet Potatoes with Brandy and Raisins

$^1/_2$ cup seedless raisins

$^1/_4$ cup brandy

4 medium sweet potatoes, boiled until just tender then peeled and sliced into $^1/_4$-inch slices

$^2/_3$ cup packed brown sugar

$^1/_4$ cup FLEISCHMANN'S® Original Margarine

2 tablespoons water

$^1/_4$ teaspoon ground cinnamon

1. Mix raisins and brandy in small bowl; let stand 20 minutes. Drain raisins.

2. Layer sweet potatoes in 9×9×2-inch baking pan; top with raisins.

3. Mix brown sugar, margarine, water and cinnamon in small saucepan; heat to a boil. Pour over sweet potatoes.

4. Bake in preheated 350°F oven for 40 minutes, basting with pan juices occasionally.   *Makes 4 to 6 servings*

Preparation Time: 20 minutes
Cook Time: 40 minutes
Total Time: 1 hour

Sweet Potatoes with Brandy and Raisins

Apple Walnut Dressing

1 bag SUCCESS® Brown Rice

1 tart green apple, cored and chopped

1 teaspoon apple-pie spice

2 tablespoons lemon juice

   Vegetable cooking spray

4 ounces bulk turkey sausage

$^3/_4$ cup chopped onion

$^1/_2$ cup chopped celery

$^1/_4$ cup chopped walnuts

$^1/_4$ cup raisins

$^1/_2$ teaspoon salt

$^1/_2$ teaspoon pepper

$^1/_8$ teaspoon dried sage

$^1/_3$ cup low-sodium chicken broth

$^1/_4$ cup honey

Prepare rice as directed on package.

Combine apple, spice and lemon juice in large bowl; mix lightly. Set aside. Spray large skillet with cooking spray. Crumble sausage into prepared skillet. Cook over medium heat until browned, stirring occasionally. Add onion, celery, walnuts and raisins; cook until crisp-tender. Add apple mixture and seasonings; cook and stir 3 minutes. Add rice, broth and honey; heat thoroughly, stirring consistently. Serve with pork or lamb chops, if desired.   *Makes 4 servings*

Festive Cranberry Mold

$^1/_2$ cup water

1 package (6 ounces) raspberry-flavored gelatin

1 can (8 ounces) cranberry sauce

1$^2/_3$ cups cranberry juice cocktail

1 cup sliced bananas (optional)

$^1/_2$ cup walnuts, toasted (optional)

In medium saucepan over medium-high heat, bring water to a boil. Add gelatin and stir until dissolved. Fold in cranberry sauce. Reduce heat to medium and cook until sauce is melted. Stir in cranberry juice cocktail.

Refrigerate mixture until slightly thickened. Fold in banana slices and walnuts, if desired. Pour mixture into 4-cup mold; cover and refrigerate until gelatin is set. *Makes 8 servings*

Festive Cranberry Mold

Green Beans with Blue Cheese and Roasted Peppers

1 bag (20 ounces) frozen cut green beans

$^1/_2$ jar (about 3 ounces) roasted red pepper strips, drained and slivered

$^1/_8$ teaspoon salt

$^1/_8$ teaspoon white pepper

4 ounces cream cheese

$^1/_2$ cup milk

$^3/_4$ cup blue cheese (3 ounces), crumbled

$^1/_2$ cup Italian-style bread crumbs

1 tablespoon margarine or butter, melted

PREHEAT oven to 350°F. Spray 2-quart oval casserole with nonstick cooking spray.

COMBINE green beans, red pepper strips, salt and pepper in prepared dish.

PLACE cream cheese and milk in small saucepan; heat over low heat, stirring until melted. Add blue cheese; stir only until combined. Pour cheese mixture over green bean mixture and stir until green beans are coated.

COMBINE bread crumbs and margarine in small bowl; sprinkle evenly over casserole.

BAKE, uncovered, 20 minutes or until hot and bubbly.

Makes 4 servings

Green Beans with Blue Cheese and Roasted Peppers

Pepperidge Farm® Sausage Corn Bread Stuffing

$^1/_4$ pound bulk pork sausage

1$^1/_4$ cups water

$^1/_2$ cup cooked whole kernel corn

$^1/_2$ cup shredded Cheddar cheese (2 ounces)

1 tablespoon chopped fresh parsley *or* 1 teaspoon dried parsley flakes

4 cups PEPPERIDGE FARM® Corn Bread Stuffing

1. In large saucepan over medium-high heat, cook sausage until browned, stirring to separate meat. Pour off fat.

2. Stir in water, corn, cheese and parsley. Add stuffing. Mix lightly. Spoon into greased 1$^1/_2$-quart casserole.

3. Cover and bake at 350°F. for 25 minutes or until hot.

Makes 6 servings

Tip: This stuffing bake brings a new flavor to the traditional holiday meal—and is easy enough for an everyday meal!

Prep Time: 15 minutes
Cook Time: 25 minutes

Roasted Garlic Mashed Potatoes

1 large bulb garlic
Olive oil
$^1/_4$ cup chopped green onions
$^1/_4$ cup margarine or butter
2$^1/_2$ pounds potatoes, peeled, cubed and cooked
1$^1/_2$ cups milk
$^1/_2$ cup GREY POUPON® Dijon Mustard
$^1/_2$ cup shredded Cheddar cheese (2 ounces)
$^1/_4$ cup chopped parsley
Salt and black pepper to taste

1. To roast garlic, peel off loose paperlike skin from bulb. Coat garlic bulb lightly with olive oil; wrap in foil. Place in small baking pan. Bake at 400°F for 40 to 45 minutes; cool. Separate cloves. Squeeze cloves to extract pulp; discard skins.

2. Cook and stir garlic pulp and green onions in margarine in large saucepan, over medium heat until tender. Add cooked potatoes, milk, mustard and cheese. Mash potato mixture until smooth and well blended. Stir in parsley; season with salt and pepper. Serve immediately.

Makes 8 servings

Orange-Glazed Carrots

1 pound fresh or thawed frozen baby carrots

1/3 cup orange marmalade

2 tablespoons butter

2 teaspoons Dijon mustard

1/2 teaspoon grated fresh ginger

Heat 1 inch lightly salted water in 2-quart saucepan over high heat to a boil; add carrots. Return to a boil. Reduce heat to low. Cover and simmer 10 to 12 minutes for fresh carrots (8 to 10 minutes for frozen carrots) or until crisp-tender. Drain well; return carrots to pan. Stir in marmalade, butter, mustard and ginger. Simmer, uncovered, over medium heat 3 minutes or until carrots are glazed, stirring occasionally.*

Makes 6 servings

At this point, carrots may be transferred to a microwavable casserole dish with lid. Cover and refrigerate up to 8 hours before serving. To reheat, microwave at HIGH (100% power) 4 to 5 minutes or until hot.

Note: Recipe may be doubled.

When buying fresh ginger, choose mature ginger that is firm with smooth tan skin and a pungent fragrance. Avoid buying ginger with wrinkled skin. This is an indication that it is past its prime.

Orange-Glazed Carrots

Wild Rice with Dried Apricots and Cranberries

$1/2$ cup uncooked wild rice

3 cups chicken broth, divided

1 cup apple juice

$3/4$ cup uncooked long-grain white rice

$1/2$ cup golden raisins

$1/2$ cup chopped dried apricots

$1/2$ cup dried cranberries

2 tablespoons butter

$3/4$ cup chopped onion

$1/2$ cup coarsely chopped pecans

$1/3$ cup chopped fresh parsley

1. Rinse wild rice in fine strainer under cold running water. Drain; set aside.

2. Combine wild rice, $1/2$ cups chicken broth and apple juice in 2-quart saucepan. Bring to a boil over medium-high heat. Reduce heat to low; simmer, covered, about 1 hour or until rice is tender. Drain; set aside.

3. Combine white rice and remaining $1/2$ cups broth in separate 2-quart saucepan. Bring to a boil over medium-high heat. Reduce heat to low; simmer, covered, 12 to 15 minutes.

4. Stir in raisins, apricots and cranberries; simmer 5 minutes or until rice is tender and fluffy and liquid is absorbed. Remove from heat. Let stand covered 5 minutes or until fruit is tender; set aside.

5. Melt butter in large skillet over medium heat. Add onion; cook and stir 5 to 6 minutes until tender. Stir in pecans. Cook and stir 2 minutes.

6. Add wild rice and white rice mixtures to skillet. Stir in parsley; cook and stir over medium heat about 2 minutes or until heated through. Garnish with fresh thyme, orange slices and whole cranberries, if desired.

Makes 6 to 8 servings

Wild Rice with Dried Apricots and Cranberries

Mashed Sweet Potatoes & Parsnips

2 large sweet potatoes (about 1¼ pounds), peeled and cut into
    1-inch pieces

2 medium parsnips (about ½ pound), peeled and cut into ½-inch
    slices

¼ cup evaporated skimmed milk

1½ tablespoons margarine or butter

½ teaspoon salt

⅛ teaspoon ground nutmeg

¼ cup chopped chives or green onion tops

1. Combine sweet potatoes and parsnips in large saucepan. Cover with cold water and bring to a boil over high heat. Reduce heat; simmer uncovered 15 minutes or until vegetables are tender.

2. Drain vegetables and return to pan. Add milk, margarine, salt and nutmeg. Mash potato mixture over low heat to desired consistency. Stir in chives. *Makes 6 servings*

Parsnips are the ivory-colored cousin to the carrot. They have a distinctly nutty and sweet flavor. Harvested in the late fall, parsnips become sweeter the

Mashed Sweet Potatoes & Parsnips

Treasury of Cakes & Pies

Bring good cheer to all with cakes and pies like Grandma use to bake. Decadent cakes, rich cheesecakes and classic pies make unforgettable endings to any meal.

Frozen Peanut Butter Pie

     Chocolate Crunch Crust (recipe follows)
1 (8-ounce) package cream cheese, softened
1 (14-ounce) can EAGLE® BRAND Sweetened Condensed Milk
     (NOT evaporated milk)
3/4 cup peanut butter
2 tablespoons REALEMON® Lemon Juice from Concentrate
1 teaspoon vanilla extract
1 cup (1/2 pint) whipping cream, whipped
     Chocolate fudge ice cream topping

1. In large mixing bowl, beat cream cheese until fluffy; gradually beat in Eagle Brand then peanut butter until smooth. Stir in ReaLemon and vanilla.

2. Fold in whipped cream. Turn into prepared crust. Drizzle topping over pie. Freeze 4 hours or until firm. Return leftovers to freezer.

Makes one 9-inch pie

Chocolate Crunch Crust: In heavy saucepan, over low heat, melt 1/3 cup margarine or butter and 1 (6-ounce) package semi-sweet chocolate chips. Remove from heat; gently stir in 2 1/2 cups oven toasted rice cereal until completely coated. Press on bottom and up side to rim of buttered 9-inch pie plate. Chill 30 minutes.

Prep Time: 20 minutes
Freeze Time: 4 hours

Maple Pumpkin Cheesecake

1 ¼ cups graham cracker crumbs

¼ cup sugar

¼ cup butter or margarine, melted

3 (8-ounce) packages cream cheese, softened

1 (14-ounce) can EAGLE® BRAND Sweetened Condensed Milk
    (NOT evaporated milk)

1 (15-ounce) can pumpkin (1 ¾ cups)

3 eggs

¼ cup maple syrup

1 ½ teaspoons ground cinnamon

1 teaspoon ground nutmeg

½ teaspoon salt

    Maple Pecan Glaze (recipe follows)

1. Preheat oven to 325°F. Combine graham cracker crumbs, sugar and butter; press firmly on bottom of 9-inch springform pan.* With mixer, beat cheese until fluffy. Gradually beat in Eagle Brand until smooth. Add pumpkin, eggs, maple syrup, cinnamon, nutmeg and salt; mix well. Pour into prepared pan. Bake 1 ¼ hours or until center appears nearly set when shaken. Cool 1 hour. Cover and chill at least 4 hours.

2. To serve, spoon some Maple Pecan Glaze over cheesecake. Garnish with whipped cream and pecans if desired. Pass remaining sauce. Store leftovers covered in refrigerator.   *Makes one (9-inch) cheesecake*

To use 13×9-inch baking pan, press crumb mixture firmly on bottom of pan. Proceed as above, except bake 50 to 60 minutes or until center appears nearly set when shaken.

Maple Pecan Glaze: In saucepan, combine ³/₄ cup maple syrup and 1 cup (¹/₂ pint) whipping cream; bring to a boil. Boil rapidly 15 to 20 minutes or until thickened; stir occasionally. Add ¹/₂ cup chopped pecans.

Prep Time: 25 minutes
Bake Time: 1 hour and 15 minutes

Maple Pumpkin Cheesecake

Very Cherry Pie

4 cups frozen unsweetened tart cherries

1 cup dried tart cherries

1 cup sugar

2 tablespoons quick-cooking tapioca

$^1/_2$ teaspoon almond extract

Pastry for double-crust 9-inch pie

$^1/_4$ teaspoon ground nutmeg

1 tablespoon butter

Combine frozen cherries, dried cherries, sugar, tapioca and almond extract in large mixing bowl; mix well. (It is not necessary to thaw cherries before using.) Let cherry mixture stand 15 minutes.

Line 9-inch pie plate with pastry; fill with cherry mixture. Sprinkle with nutmeg. Dot with butter. Cover with top crust, cutting slits for steam to escape. Or, cut top crust into strips for lattice top and cherry leaf cutouts.

Bake in preheated 375°F oven about 1 hour or until crust is golden brown and filling is bubbly. If necessary, cover edge of crust with foil to prevent overbrowning. *Makes 8 servings*

Note: Two (16-ounce) cans unsweetened tart cherries, well drained, can be substituted for frozen tart cherries. Dried cherries are available at gourmet and specialty food stores and at selected supermarkets.

Favorite recipe from **Cherry Marketing Institute**

Very Cherry Pie

Planters® Perfect Pecan Pie

3 eggs

1 cup light corn syrup

1 cup sugar

2 tablespoons margarine or butter, melted

1 teaspoon vanilla extract

$^{1}/_{8}$ teaspoon salt

1 cup PLANTERS® Pecan Halves

1 (9-inch) unbaked pastry shell

Whipped cream and PLANTERS® Pecan Halves, for garnish

1. Beat eggs slightly. Stir in corn syrup, sugar, margarine or butter, vanilla and salt until blended.

2. Stir in pecan halves; pour into pastry shell.

3. Bake at 400°F for 15 minutes. Reduce temperature to 350°F, bake for 25 to 30 minutes more or until lightly browned and completely puffed across top. Cool completely.

4. Serve garnished with whipped cream and pecan halves if desired.

Makes 8 servings

Treat your family and friends to a slice of this decadent pie. Serve with hot coffee and a scoop of cinnamon ice cream for a fantastic end to any meal.

Holiday Fruit Cake

1 (16-ounce) package HONEY MAID® Honey Graham, finely
    rolled (about 5 cups crumbs)
$^{1}/_{2}$ teaspoon ground cinnamon
$^{1}/_{2}$ teaspoon ground allspice
$^{1}/_{4}$ teaspoon ground cloves
$^{3}/_{4}$ cup seedless raisins
  1 cup pitted dates, snipped
12 ounces (about $1^{1}/_{2}$ cups) mixed candied fruit
  1 cup PLANTERS® Walnut Pieces, chopped
$^{1}/_{2}$ cup orange juice
$^{1}/_{3}$ cup light corn syrup

1. Mix crumbs, cinnamon, allspice, cloves, raisins, dates, candied fruit and walnuts in large bowl.

2. Blend orange juice and corn syrup in small bowl; add to crumb mixture, blending until moistened. Press firmly into foil-lined $8^{1}/_{2}\times4^{1}/_{2}\times2^{1}/_{2}$-inch loaf pan; cover tightly. Store at least 2 days in refrigerator before serving. Cake will keep several weeks in refrigerator.

Makes 1 (8-inch) loaf

Chocolate Cake Squares with Eggnog Sauce

$1\frac{1}{2}$ teaspoons baking soda

1 cup buttermilk or sour milk*

$\frac{3}{4}$ cup HERSHEY'S Cocoa

$\frac{3}{4}$ cup boiling water

$\frac{1}{4}$ cup ($\frac{1}{2}$ stick) butter or margarine, softened

$\frac{1}{4}$ cup shortening

2 cups sugar

2 eggs

1 teaspoon vanilla extract

$\frac{1}{8}$ teaspoon salt

$1\frac{3}{4}$ cups all-purpose flour

Eggnog Sauce (recipe follows)

*To sour milk: Use 1 tablespoon white vinegar plus milk to equal 1 cup.

1. Heat oven to 350°F. Grease and flour 13×9×2-inch baking pan.

2. Stir baking soda into buttermilk in medium bowl; set aside. Stir together cocoa and water until smooth; set aside.

3. Beat butter, shortening and sugar in large bowl until creamy. Add eggs, vanilla and salt; beat well. Add buttermilk mixture alternately with flour to butter mixture, beating until blended. Add cocoa mixture; blend thoroughly. Pour batter into prepared pan.

4. Bake 40 to 45 minutes or until wooden pick inserted in center comes out clean. Cool completely. Serve with Eggnog Sauce.

Makes 12 to 15 servings

Eggnog Sauce

   1 tablespoon cornstarch

   2 tablespoons cold water

   1 $\frac{1}{3}$ cups milk

   $\frac{1}{4}$ cup sugar

   3 egg yolks, beaten

   $\frac{1}{4}$ teaspoon *each* brandy and vanilla extracts

   Several dashes ground nutmeg

1. Stir cornstarch and water in saucepan until smooth. Add milk, sugar and egg yolks. Beat with whisk until well blended. Cook over medium heat, stirring constantly, until thickened. Remove from heat. Stir in extracts. Cool completely. Sprinkle nutmeg over top.

Makes about 1$\frac{3}{4}$ cups sauce

Chocolate Cake Square with Eggnog Sauce

Double Layer Pumpkin Pie

1/2 package (4 ounces) PHILADELPHIA® Cream Cheese, cubed,
   softened
1 tablespoon half-and-half or milk
1 tablespoon sugar
1 tub (8 ounces) COOL WHIP® Whipped Topping, thawed
1 prepared graham cracker crumb crust (6 ounces)
1 cup cold half-and-half or milk
2 packages (4-serving size) JELL-O® Vanilla Flavor Instant
   Pudding & Pie Filling
1 can (16 ounces) pumpkin
1 teaspoon ground cinnamon
1/2 teaspoon ground ginger
1/4 teaspoon ground cloves

BEAT cream cheese, 1 tablespoon half-and-half and sugar in large bowl with wire whisk until smooth. Gently stir in 1 1/2 cups of the whipped topping. Spread onto bottom of crust.

POUR 1 cup half-and-half into bowl. Add pudding mixes. Beat with wire whisk 1 minute. (Mixture will be thick.) Stir in pumpkin and spices with wire whisk until well blended. Spread over cream cheese layer.

REFRIGERATE 4 hours or until set. Garnish with remaining whipped topping and sprinkle with additional cinnamon.   *Makes 8 servings*

Double Layer Chocolate Pie: Omit pumpkin and spices, and increase half-and-half to 1 1/2 cups. Prepare recipe as directed, substituting JELL-O® Chocolate Flavor Instant Pudding for vanilla pudding.

Double Layer Pumpkin Pie

Chocolate and White Yule Log

4 eggs, separated and at room temperature

$^1/_2$ cup plus $^1/_3$ cup sugar, divided

1 teaspoon vanilla extract

$^1/_2$ cup all-purpose flour

$^1/_4$ cup HERSHEY'S Cocoa

$^1/_2$ teaspoon baking powder

$^1/_4$ teaspoon baking soda

$^1/_8$ teaspoon salt

$^1/_3$ cup water

White Cream Filling (recipe follows)

Chocolate Glaze (recipe follows)

1. Heat oven to 375°F. Line $15^1/_2 \times 10^1/_2 \times 1$-inch jelly roll pan with foil; generously grease foil.

2. Beat egg whites in large bowl until soft peaks form; gradually add $^1/_2$ cup sugar, a tablespoon at a time, beating on high speed of mixer until stiff peaks form. Beat egg yolks and vanilla in medium bowl on high speed about 3 minutes; gradually add remaining $^1/_3$ cup sugar. Continue beating 2 additional minutes until mixture is thick and lemon-colored.

3. Stir together flour, cocoa, baking powder, baking soda and salt; gently fold into egg yolk mixture alternately with water just until mixture is smooth. Gradually fold chocolate mixture into egg whites; spread batter evenly into prepared pan.

4. Bake 12 to 15 minutes or until top springs back when touched lightly in center. Immediately loosen cake from edges of pan; invert onto linen towel sprinkled with powdered sugar. Carefully peel off foil. Immediately roll cake in towel starting from narrow end; place on wire rack. Cool.

5. Prepare White Cream Filling. Unroll cake; remove towel. Spread with filling; reroll cake. Spread Chocolate Glaze over top and sides. Cover; refrigerate until just before serving. Cover; refrigerate leftover dessert.

Makes 10 to 12 servings

White Cream Filling

$^1/_2$ teaspoon unflavored gelatin
1 tablespoon cold water
$^2/_3$ cup HERSHEY'S Premier White Chips
$^1/_4$ cup milk
1 teaspoon vanilla extract
1 cup ($^1/_2$ pint) cold whipping cream

1. Sprinkle gelatin over cold water in cup; let stand 1 minute to soften.

2. Combine white chips and milk in small microwave-safe bowl. Microwave at HIGH (100%) 30 seconds to 1 minute; stir after 30 seconds, until chips are melted and mixture is smooth when stirred. Add gelatin mixture and vanilla; stir until gelatin is dissolved. Cool to room temperature.

3. Beat whipping cream in small bowl until stiff; carefully fold into chip mixture. Refrigerate 10 minutes or until filling begins to set.

Makes about 2 cups filling

Chocolate Glaze: Melt 2 tablespoons butter in small saucepan over low heat; add 2 tablespoons HERSHEY'S Cocoa and 2 tablespoons water, stirring until smooth and slightly thickened. Do not boil. Remove from heat; cool slightly. Gradually add 1 cup powdered sugar and $^1/_2$ teaspoon vanilla extract; beat with whisk until smooth. If necessary, add additional water, a few drops at a time, until of desired consistency.

Glazed Cranberry Mini-Cakes

$1/3$ cup butter or margarine, softened

$1/3$ cup granulated sugar

$1/3$ cup packed light brown sugar

1 egg

$1 1/4$ teaspoons vanilla extract

$1 1/3$ cups all-purpose flour

$3/4$ teaspoon baking powder

$1/4$ teaspoon baking soda

$1/4$ teaspoon salt

2 tablespoons milk

$1 1/4$ cups coarsely chopped fresh cranberries

$1/2$ cup coarsely chopped walnuts

$1 2/3$ cups HERSHEY'S Premier White Chips, divided

White Glaze (recipe follows)

1. Heat oven to 350°F. Lightly grease or paper-line small muffin cups ($1 3/4$ inches in diameter).

2. Beat butter, granulated sugar, brown sugar, egg and vanilla in large bowl until fluffy. Stir together flour, baking powder, baking soda and salt; gradually blend into butter mixture. Add milk; stir until blended. Stir in cranberries, walnuts and $2/3$ cup white chips (reserve remaining chips for glaze). Fill muffin cups $7/8$ full with batter.

3. Bake 18 to 20 minutes or until wooden pick inserted in center comes out clean. Cool 5 minutes; remove from pans to wire rack. Cool completely. Prepare White Glaze; drizzle over top of mini-cakes. Refrigerate 10 minutes to set glaze.   *Makes about 3 dozen mini-cakes*

White Glaze: Place remaining 1 cup HERSHEY'S Premier White Chips in small microwave-safe bowl; sprinkle 2 tablespoons vegetable oil over chips. Microwave at HIGH (100% power) 30 seconds; stir. If necessary, microwave at HIGH additional 30 seconds or just until chips are melted when stirred.

Glazed Cranberry Mini-Cakes

Old-Fashioned Gingerbread

2 tablespoons margarine, melted and cooled

1/3 cup packed brown sugar

1/4 cup cholesterol-free egg substitute

1/4 cup buttermilk

2 cups all-purpose flour

1 1/2 teaspoons baking soda

1 1/2 teaspoons ground ginger

1 teaspoon ground cinnamon

1/2 teaspoon salt

1 tablespoon instant decaffeinated coffee granules

1 cup hot water

1/2 cup molasses

1/4 cup honey

1 jar (2 1/2 ounces) puréed prunes

Reduced fat nondairy whipped topping (optional)

1. Preheat oven to 350°F. Spray 9-inch square or 11×7-inch baking pan with nonstick cooking spray; set aside.

2. Combine margarine, brown sugar, egg substitute and buttermilk in medium bowl; set aside. Combine flour, baking soda, ginger, cinnamon and salt in large bowl; set aside. Dissolve coffee granules in hot water in small bowl. Stir in molasses, honey and puréed prunes.

3. Add flour mixture alternately with coffee mixture to margarine mixture. Batter will be lumpy. Do not over mix.

4. Pour batter into prepared pan. Bake 40 to 45 minutes or until wooden pick inserted in center comes out clean. Cool in pan on wire rack. Before serving, top with whipped topping, if desired.   *Makes 8 servings*

Old-Fashioned Gingerbread

Best-Ever Apple Pie

2$^{1}/_{3}$ cups all-purpose flour, divided

$^{3}/_{4}$ cup plus 1 tablespoon sugar, divided

$^{1}/_{2}$ teaspoon baking powder

$^{1}/_{2}$ teaspoon salt

$^{3}/_{4}$ cup plus 3 tablespoons cold unsalted butter, cut into small pieces, divided

4 to 5 tablespoons ice water

1 egg, separated

7 medium tart apples, peeled, cored and sliced

1 tablespoon lemon juice

1$^{1}/_{4}$ teaspoons ground cinnamon

1 tablespoon sour cream

1. Combine 2 cups flour, 1 tablespoon sugar, baking powder and salt in large bowl until well blended. Cut in $^{3}/_{4}$ cup butter using pastry blender or 2 knives until mixture resembles coarse crumbs. Add water, 1 tablespoon at a time, to flour mixture. Toss with fork until mixture holds together. Form dough into 2 discs. Wrap discs in plastic wrap; refrigerate 30 minutes or until firm.

2. Working with 1 disc at a time, roll out dough on lightly floured surface with lightly floured rolling pin into 12-inch circle, $^{1}/_{8}$ inch thick. Ease dough into 9-inch glass pie plate. *Do not stretch dough.* Trim dough leaving $^{1}/_{2}$-inch overhang; brush with egg white. Set aside.

3. Preheat oven to 450°F. Place apple slices in large bowl; sprinkle with lemon juice. Combine remaining $^{1}/_{3}$ cup flour, $^{3}/_{4}$ cup sugar and cinnamon in small bowl until well blended. Add to apple mixture; toss to coat. Spoon filling into prepared pie crust; place remaining 3 tablespoons butter on top of filling.

4. Moisten edge of dough with water. Roll out remaining disc. Place onto filled pie. Trim dough leaving $^1/_2$-inch overhang. Flute edge. Cut slits in dough at $^1/_2$-inch intervals around edge to form flaps. Press 1 flap in toward center of pie and the next out toward rim of pie plate. Continue around edge. Cut 4 small slits in top of dough to allow steam to escape.

5. Combine egg yolk and sour cream in small bowl until well blended. Cover; refrigerate until ready to use.

6. Bake 10 minutes; *reduce oven temperature to 375°F.* Bake 35 minutes. Brush egg yolk mixture evenly on pie crust with pastry brush. Bake 20 to 25 minutes or until crust is deep golden brown. Cool completely on wire rack.   *Makes one (9-inch) pie*

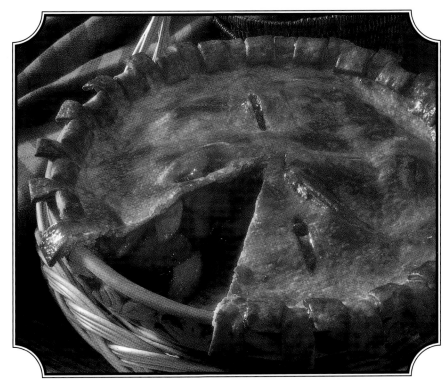

Best-Ever Apple Pie

Sleighful of Cookies & Candies

'Tis the season for everyone's favorite cookies and candies. Pack a tin full of a taste-tempting assortment for the perfect hostess gift.

Holiday Cheesecake Presents

1 1/2 cups graham cracker crumbs

1/3 cup butter *or* margarine, melted

3 tablespoons sugar

3 packages (8 ounces each) PHILADELPHIA® Cream Cheese,
softened

3/4 cup sugar

1 teaspoon vanilla

3 eggs

MIX crumbs, butter and 3 tablespoons sugar; press onto bottom of
13×9-inch baking pan.

MIX cream cheese, 3/4 cup sugar and vanilla with electric mixer on
medium speed until well blended. Add eggs; mix until blended. Pour over
crust.

BAKE at 350°F for 30 minutes or until center is almost set. Cool.
Refrigerate 3 hours or overnight. Cut into bars. Decorate bars with
decorating gels and sprinkles to resemble presents. Store leftover bars in
refrigerator.   *Makes 2 dozen bars*

Prep Time: 10 minutes plus refrigerating
Bake Time: 30 minutes

Mocha Rum Balls

60 NILLA® Wafers, finely rolled (about 2¹/₂ cups crumbs)
1 cup powdered sugar
1 cup PLANTERS® Pecans, finely chopped
¹/₂ cup margarine or butter, melted
2 tablespoons light corn syrup
2 tablespoons unsweetened cocoa
¹/₄ cup rum
1 teaspoon instant coffee granules
Powdered sugar, for coating

1. Mix crumbs, 1 cup powdered sugar, pecans, melted margarine or butter, corn syrup and cocoa in large bowl. Blend rum and instant coffee until coffee granules are dissolved; stir into crumb mixture. Let stand 15 minutes.

2. Shape mixture into 1-inch balls; roll in additional powdered sugar. Store in airtight container, separating layers with waxed paper. Flavor improves with standing. *Makes about 3 dozen*

Preparation Time: 50 minutes
Total Time: 50 minutes

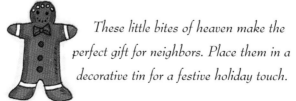

These little bites of heaven make the perfect gift for neighbors. Place them in a decorative tin for a festive holiday touch.

Top to bottom: Holiday Truffles (page 100) and Mocha Rum Balls

Date Pinwheel Cookies

1¼ cups dates, pitted and finely chopped

¾ cup orange juice

½ cup granulated sugar

1 tablespoon butter

3 cups plus 1 tablespoon all-purpose flour, divided

2 teaspoons vanilla, divided

4 ounces cream cheese

¼ cup shortening

1 cup packed brown sugar

2 eggs

1 teaspoon baking soda

½ teaspoon salt

1. Heat dates, orange juice, granulated sugar, butter and 1 tablespoon flour in medium saucepan over medium heat. Cook 10 minutes or until thick, stirring frequently; remove from heat. Stir in 1 teaspoon vanilla; set aside to cool.

2. Beat cream cheese, shortening and brown sugar about 3 minutes in large bowl until light and fluffy. Add eggs and remaining 1 teaspoon vanilla; beat 2 minutes longer.

3. Combine 3 cups flour, baking soda and salt in medium bowl. Add to shortening mixture; stir just until blended. Divide dough in half. Roll one half of dough on lightly floured work surface into 12×9-inch rectangle. Spread half of date mixture over dough. Spread evenly, leaving ¼-inch border at top short edge. Starting at short side, tightly roll up dough jelly-roll style. Wrap in plastic wrap; freeze for at least 1 hour. Repeat with remaining dough.

4. Preheat oven to 350°F. Grease cookie sheets. Unwrap dough. Using heavy thread or dental floss, cut dough into ¼-inch slices. Place slices 1 inch apart on prepared cookie sheets.

5. Bake 12 minutes or until lightly browned. Let cookies stand on cookie sheets 2 minutes. Remove cookies to wire rack; cool completely.

Makes 6 dozen cookies

Date Pinwheel Cookies

Holiday Truffles

3 tablespoons heavy cream
1 tablespoon instant coffee granules
2 cups semisweet or milk chocolate chips
1/2 cup FLEISCHMANN'S® Original Margarine
1 teaspoon vanilla extract
Crushed cookie crumbs, chopped nuts, toasted coconut, melted
white chocolate, colored sprinkles

1. Blend heavy cream and coffee in small bowl; let stand 5 minutes to dissolve.

2. Melt chocolate chips in medium saucepan over low heat until smooth. Remove from heat. With wire whisk, beat in margarine, heavy cream mixture and vanilla until smooth. Place in bowl; refrigerate until firm, about 3 hours.

3. Shape teaspoonfuls of mixture into balls and coat with cookie crumbs, chopped nuts, coconut, melted white chocolate or colored sprinkles until well coated. Store in airtight container in refrigerator.

Makes 2 1/2 dozen

Prep Time: 30 minutes
Cook Time: 5 minutes
Chill Time: 3 hours
Total Time: 3 hours and 35 minutes

Traditional Christmas Fudge

    2 tablespoons butter or margarine
$^2/_3$ cup undiluted CARNATION® Evaporated Milk
1$^1/_2$ cups granulated sugar
 $^1/_4$ teaspoon salt
    2 cups (4 ounces) miniature marshmallows
1$^1/_2$ cups (9 ounces) NESTLÉ® TOLL HOUSE® Semi-Sweet
        Chocolate Morsels
 $^1/_2$ cup chopped pecans or walnuts
    1 teaspoon vanilla extract

COMBINE butter, evaporated milk, sugar and salt in medium, heavy saucepan. Bring to a boil over medium heat, stirring constantly. Boil for 4 to 5 minutes, stirring constantly. Remove from heat.

STIR in marshmallows, morsels, nuts and vanilla. Stir vigorously for 1 minute or until marshmallows are melted. Pour into foil-lined 8-inch square baking pan. Sprinkle with additional pecans if desired. Chill until firm. Cut into pieces.   *Makes about 2 pounds*

Milk Chocolate Fudge: Substitute 2 cups (11$^1/_2$-ounce package) NESTLÉ® TOLL HOUSE® Milk Chocolate Morsels for Semi-Sweet Morsels.

Butterscotch Fudge: Substitute 2 cups (12-ounce package) NESTLÉ® TOLL HOUSE® Butterscotch Flavored Morsels for Semi-Sweet Morsels.

Mint Chocolate Fudge: Substitute 1$^1/_2$ cups (10-ounce package) NESTLÉ® TOLL HOUSE® Mint-Chocolate Morsels for Semi-Sweet Morsels.

Norwegian Wreaths

>   1 hard-cooked large egg yolk
>   1 large egg, separated
> $^1/_2$ cup butter, softened
> $^1/_2$ cup powdered sugar
> $^1/_2$ teaspoon vanilla
> 1 $^1/_4$ cups all-purpose flour
>   Coarse sugar crystals or crushed sugar cubes

1. Preheat oven to 350°F. Grease cookie sheets; set aside.

2. Beat cooked and raw egg yolks in medium bowl until smooth. Beat in butter, powdered sugar and vanilla. Stir in 1 cup flour. Stir in additional flour until stiff dough forms.

3. Place dough on sheet of waxed paper. Using waxed paper to hold dough, roll it back and forth to form a log; cut into 18 equal pieces. Roll each piece of dough into an 8-inch rope, tapering ends.

4. Shape ropes into wreaths; overlap ends and let extend out from wreath. Place wreaths on prepared cookie sheets. Refrigerate 15 minutes or until firm.

5. Beat reserved egg white with fork until foamy. Brush wreaths with egg white; sprinkle with sugar crystals. Bake 8 to 10 minutes or until light golden brown. Remove cookies to wire racks; cool completely.

Makes about 1 $^1/_2$ dozen cookies

Norwegian Wreaths

Stained Glass Cookies

$^1/_2$ cup margarine or butter, softened

$^1/_2$ cup sugar

$^1/_2$ cup honey

$^1/_4$ cup egg substitute

1 teaspoon vanilla extract

3 cups all-purpose flour

1 teaspoon DAVIS® Baking Powder

$^1/_2$ teaspoon baking soda

$^1/_2$ teaspoon salt

5 (.90-ounce) rolls Five Flavor or Fancy Fruits LIFE SAVERS® Candy

1. Beat together margarine or butter, sugar, honey, egg substitute and vanilla in bowl with mixer until creamy. Mix in flour, baking powder, baking soda and salt. Cover; refrigerate at least 2 hours.

2. Roll dough on lightly floured surface to $^1/_4$-inch thickness. Cut dough into desired shapes with $2^1/_2$- to 3-inch floured cookie cutters. Trace smaller version of cookie shape on dough leaving $^1/_2$- to $^3/_4$-inch border of dough. Cut out and remove dough from center of cookies; set aside. Place cut-out shapes on baking sheets lined with foil. Repeat with reserved dough, re-rolling scraps as necessary.

3. Crush each color of candy separately between two layers of wax paper. Spoon crushed candy inside centers of cut-out cookie shapes.

4. Bake in preheated 350°F oven for 6 to 8 minutes or until candy is melted and cookies are lightly browned. Cool cookies completely before removing from foil. *Makes 3¹/₂ dozen cookies*

Prep Time: 1 hour
Chill Time: 2 hours
Cook Time: 6 minutes
Total Time: 3 hours and 6 minutes

Stained Glass Cookies

Holiday Peppermint Candies

$^1/_2$ package (4 ounces) PHILADELPHIA® Cream Cheese, softened
1 tablespoon butter *or* margarine
1 tablespoon light corn syrup
$^1/_4$ teaspoon peppermint extract *or* few drops peppermint oil
4 cups powdered sugar
　Green and red food coloring
　Sifted powdered sugar
　Green, red and white decorating icing (optional)

MIX cream cheese, butter, corn syrup and extract in large mixing bowl with electric mixer on medium speed until well blended. Gradually add 4 cups powdered sugar; mix well.

DIVIDE mixture into thirds. Knead a few drops green food coloring into first third; repeat with red food coloring and second third. Wrap each third in plastic wrap.

SHAPE into 1-inch balls, working with 1 color mixture at a time. Place on wax paper-lined cookie sheet. Flatten each ball with bottom of glass that has been lightly dipped in sifted powdered sugar.

REPEAT with remaining mixtures. Decorate with icing. Store candies in refrigerator. *Makes 5 dozen*

Prep Time: 30 minutes plus refrigerating

112

Holiday Peppermint Candies

113

Classic Peanut Brittle

MAZOLA NO STICK® Cooking Spray
1 cup KARO® Light or Dark Corn Syrup
1 cup sugar
1/4 cup water
2 tablespoons margarine or butter
1 1/2 cups peanuts
1 teaspoon baking soda

1. Spray large cookie sheet and metal spatula with cooking spray; set aside.

2. In heavy 3-quart saucepan combine corn syrup, sugar, water and margarine. Stirring constantly, cook over medium heat until sugar dissolves and mixture comes to boil.

3. Without stirring, cook until temperature reaches 280°F on candy thermometer or small amount of mixture dropped into very cold water separates into threads which are hard but not brittle.

4. Gradually stir in peanuts. Stirring frequently, continue cooking until temperature reaches 300°F or small amount of mixture dropped into very cold water separates into threads which are hard and brittle. Remove from heat; stir in baking soda.

5. Immediately pour mixture onto cookie sheet. With metal spatula, spread mixture evenly to edges. Cool. Break into pieces.

Makes about 1 1/2 pounds

Prep Time: 60 minutes, plus cooling

Gingerbread Cookies

3/4 cup light or dark molasses

3/4 cup margarine or butter

3/4 cup packed light brown sugar

4 1/2 cups all-purpose flour

1 tablespoon ground ginger

2 teaspoons ground cinnamon

1 teaspoon DAVIS® Baking Powder

1/2 teaspoon baking soda

1/2 teaspoon ground nutmeg

1/4 cup egg substitute

Decorator icing, raisins and assorted candies, optional

1. Heat molasses, margarine or butter and brown sugar in saucepan over medium heat to a boil, stirring occasionally. Remove from heat; cool.

2. Mix flour, ginger, cinnamon, baking powder, baking soda and nutmeg in large bowl. Blend egg substitute into molasses mixture. Stir molasses mixture into flour mixture until smooth. Wrap dough; refrigerate 1 hour.

3. Divide dough in half. Roll dough to 1/4-inch thickness on floured surface. Cut with floured 5×3-inch gingerbread people cutters. Place on lightly greased baking sheets.

4. Bake in preheated 350°F oven for 10 to 12 minutes or until lightly browned. Remove from sheets; cool on wire racks. Decorate as desired with icing, raisins and candies. *Makes 2 dozen cookies*

Raspberry Almond Sandwich Cookies

1 package DUNCAN HINES® Golden Sugar Cookie Mix
1 egg
1/4 cup vegetable oil
1 tablespoon water
3/4 teaspoon almond extract
1 1/3 cups sliced natural almonds, broken
Seedless red raspberry jam

Preheat oven to 375°F.

Combine cookie mix, egg, oil, water and almond extract in large bowl. Stir until thoroughly blended. Drop half of dough by level teaspoonfuls 2 inches apart onto *ungreased* cookie sheets. (Dough will spread during baking to 1 1/2 to 1 3/4 inches.)

Place almonds on waxed paper. Drop remaining half of dough by level teaspoonfuls onto nuts. Place almond side up 2 inches apart on *ungreased* cookie sheets.

Bake both plain and almond cookies 6 minutes or until set but not browned. Cool 1 minute on cookie sheets. Remove to cooling racks. Cool completely.

Spread bottoms of plain cookies with jam; top with almond cookies. Press together to make sandwiches. Store in airtight container.

Makes 6 dozen sandwich cookies

Raspberry Almond Sandwich Cookies

117

Two-Toned Spritz Cookies

1 square (1 ounce) unsweetened chocolate, coarsely chopped

1 cup (2 sticks) butter, softened

1 cup sugar

1 egg

1 teaspoon vanilla

2¼ cups all-purpose flour

¼ teaspoon salt

Melt chocolate in small, heavy saucepan over low heat, stirring constantly; set aside. Beat butter and sugar in large bowl until light and fluffy. Beat in egg and vanilla. Combine flour and salt in medium bowl; gradually add to butter mixture. Reserve 2 cups dough. Beat chocolate into dough in bowl until smooth. Cover both doughs and refrigerate until firm enough to handle, about 20 minutes.

Preheat oven to 400°F. Roll out vanilla dough between two sheets of waxed paper to ½-inch thickness. Cut into 5×4-inch rectangles. Place chocolate dough on sheet of waxed paper. Using waxed paper to hold dough, roll back and forth to form a log about 1 inch in diameter. Cut into 5-inch-long logs. Place chocolate log in center of vanilla rectangle. Wrap vanilla dough around log and fit into cookie press fitted with star disc. Press dough onto *ungreased* cookie sheets 1½ inches apart. Bake about 10 minutes or until just set. Remove cookies with spatula to wire racks; cool completely. *Makes about 4 dozen cookies*

118

Two-Toned Spritz Cookies

Raspberry Pecan Thumbprints

    2 cups all-purpose flour
    1 cup pecan pieces, finely chopped and divided
 $^{1}/_{2}$ teaspoon ground cinnamon
 $^{1}/_{4}$ teaspoon ground allspice
 $^{1}/_{8}$ teaspoon salt
    1 cup butter, softened
 $^{1}/_{2}$ cup packed light brown sugar
    2 teaspoons vanilla
 $^{1}/_{3}$ cup seedless raspberry jam

Preheat oven to 350°F. Combine flour, $^{1}/_{2}$ cup pecans, cinnamon, allspice and salt in medium bowl.

Beat butter in large bowl until smooth. Gradually beat in sugar; beat until light and fluffy. Beat in vanilla until blended. Beat in flour mixture just until blended.

Form dough into 1-inch balls; flatten slightly and place on ungreased cookie sheets. Press down with thumb in center of each ball to form indentation. Pinch together any cracks in dough. Fill each indentation with generous $^{1}/_{4}$ teaspoon jam. Sprinkle filled cookies with remaining $^{1}/_{2}$ cup pecans.

Bake 14 minutes or until just set. Let cookies stand on cookie sheets 5 minutes; transfer to wire racks to cool completely. Store in airtight container at room temperature. Cookies are best day after baking.

Makes 3 dozen cookies

Raspberry Pecan Thumbprints

ACKNOWLEDGMENTS

The publisher would like to thank the companies and organizations listed below for the use of their recipes and photographs in this publication.

Bestfoods

Bob Evans®

Campbell Soup Company

Cherry Marketing Institute

DAVIS® Baking Powder

Dole Food Company, Inc.

Duncan Hines® and Moist Deluxe® are registered trademarks of Aurora Foods Inc.

Eagle® Brand

Equal® sweetener

Fleischmann's® Original Spread

Grey Poupon® Dijon Mustard

Hershey Foods Corporation

HONEY MAID® Honey Grahams

The Kingsford Products Company

Kraft Foods Holdings

Lawry's® Foods, Inc.

Lipton®

McIlhenny Company (TABASCO® brand Pepper Sauce)

Nabisco Biscuit Company

National Fisheries Institute

Nestlé USA, Inc.

NILLA® Wafers

Perdue Farms Incorporated

PLANTERS® Nuts

Reckitt Benckiser

Riviana Foods Inc.

VOLUME MEASUREMENTS (dry)

1/8 teaspoon = 0.5 mL
1/4 teaspoon = 1 mL
1/2 teaspoon = 2 mL
3/4 teaspoon = 4 mL
1 teaspoon = 5 mL
1 tablespoon = 15 mL
2 tablespoons = 30 mL
1/4 cup = 60 mL
1/3 cup = 75 mL
1/2 cup = 125 mL
2/3 cup = 150 mL
3/4 cup = 175 mL
1 cup = 250 mL
2 cups = 1 pint = 500 mL
3 cups = 750 mL
4 cups = 1 quart = 1 L

VOLUME MEASUREMENTS (fluid)

1 fluid ounce (2 tablespoons) = 30 mL
4 fluid ounces (1/2 cup) = 125 mL
8 fluid ounces (1 cup) = 250 mL
12 fluid ounces (1 1/2 cups) = 375 mL
16 fluid ounces (2 cups) = 500 mL

WEIGHTS (mass)

1/2 ounce = 15 g
1 ounce = 30 g
3 ounces = 90 g
4 ounces = 120 g
8 ounces = 225 g
10 ounces = 285 g
12 ounces = 360 g
16 ounces = 1 pound = 450 g

DIMENSIONS

1/16 inch = 2 mm
1/8 inch = 3 mm
1/4 inch = 6 mm
1/2 inch = 1.5 cm
3/4 inch = 2 cm
1 inch = 2.5 cm

OVEN TEMPERATURES

250°F = 120°C
275°F = 140°C
300°F = 150°C
325°F = 160°C
350°F = 180°C
375°F = 190°C
400°F = 200°C
425°F = 220°C
450°F = 230°C

BAKING PAN SIZES

Utensil	Size in Inches/Quarts	Metric Volume	Size in Centimeters
Baking or	8×8×2	2 L	20×20×5
Cake Pan	9×9×2	2.5 L	23×23×5
(square or	12×8×2	3 L	30×20×5
rectangular)	13×9×2	3.5 L	33×23×5
Loaf Pan	8×4×3	1.5 L	20×10×7
	9×5×3	2 L	23×13×7
Round Layer	8×1½	1.2 L	20×4
Cake Pan	9×1½	1.5 L	23×4
Pie Plate	8×1¼	750 mL	20×3
	9×1¼	1 L	23×3
Baking Dish	1 quart	1 L	—
or Casserole	1½ quart	1.5 L	—
	2 quart	2 L	—